C000230529

A Book of Saints and Heroines

A BOOK OF SAINTS AND HEROINES

JOANNA BOGLE

GRACEWING

First published in England in 2013
by
Gracewing
2 Southern Avenue
Leominster
Herefordshire HR6 0QF
United Kingdom
www.gracewing.co.uk

No part of this publication may be reproduced, stored in a
retrieval system, or transmitted in any form or by any means,
electronic, mechanical, photocopying, recording or otherwise,
without the written permission of the publisher.

The right of Joanna Bogle to be identified
as the author of this work has been asserted in accordance
with the Copyright, Designs and Patents Act 1988.

© 2013 Joanna Bogle

ISBN 978 085244 810 6

Typeset by Gracewing

Cover design by Bernardita Peña Hurtado

CONTENTS

INTRODUCTION

s YOU GO through this book, you will see how, down through all the 2,000 years of the Church there have been women who have loved Christ and served the human family. They have been mothers and teachers, visionaries and mystics, women who served the poor, women who held public office, women making big decisions, women who showed extraordinary courage as martyrs enduring imprisonment and death.

There has never been a time in the Church when women have not been active and faithful. Of course there have been a great many who were really saints but who never became famous. When the Church declares someone a saint, it is a way of showing honour that will also reflect on other people too.

There are two ways to read this book: one is to start at the beginning, with Mary, the Mother of Christ, and work through, reading about the women who, century by century, did great things for God. Another way is simply to dip in, and dart about, reading the different stories at random.

Either way, it is important to understand that Jesus Christ was born at a particular place and time, in Bethlehem two thousand years ago, and that since then the Christian Faith has been taken to every corner of the world, and is still being taught. Some parts of the world, like the southern parts of Africa, only received the message from missionaries quite recently, others received it long ago and have churches and schools and shrines that are very old indeed. It is saints who sustain and spread the Faith, and today we need plenty of saints so that great things can be done. There are many adventures ahead, and there are so many people who need to know about God's love, and to be loved and helped by saints and heroines. Wherever there are people who are lonely or frightened, or children who need to be given a chance of a good education, or people living under injustice, or gravely ill people who need proper care, or desperately poor people who need food and shelter, we need saints and heroines to give help and service.

Joanna Bogle
15 August 2013, Solemnity of the Assumption

1

MARY, THE MOTHER OF THE LORD

NY BOOK ON saints and heroines must start with Mary, the daughter of Sion whose "Yes" to God brought about the Incarnation. Mary is the central figure who links the Old Testament with the New.

Mary was a young woman, belonging to the family line of King David, living in the small village of Nazareth. She was betrothed to Joseph, and they had both entrusted their lives to God.

For centuries and centuries, the Jewish people had awaited the coming of the Messiah. God had chosen Abraham long before, and established a covenant with him, promising him that he would be the father of a great nation. Faithfully, since that time, God had kept his word. He gave his chosen people, the Jews, kings and prophets. Using Moses to guide them, he led them safely out of slavery in Egypt. He fed them manna in the desert, and brought them finally to their own land.

Now he was to bring his promises to fulfilment. He sent his angel, Gabriel, to the Jewish maiden, Mary, to ask her if she would co-operate in his great saving plan. At first she was puzzled when she learned that she would have a child, for she was a virgin. But the angel told her that this would all happen through the

Holy Spirit. She responded with faith and love: "I am the handmaid of the Lord".

Mary was to be the mother of God's own son, Jesus Christ, the Saviour of the world. He would be conceived in her womb by the Holy Spirit, and cradled in Mary's womb, he would be born at Bethlehem. In full unity with his Father and the Holy Spirit, he would redeem mankind from sin and open up the door to Heaven for all who chose to enter.

Mary's "Yes" to God's plan required courage. As the events progressed, she would learn again and again just how much courage. On the night of Christ's birth, there was no room at the inn and so he was born in a stable. The local tyrant ruler, Herod, was angry and jealous at learning of the birth of a king and sent out his troops to kill all the baby boys in the district — Mary and Joseph escaped with the child to Egypt.

At the Presentation of the infant Christ in the Temple at Jerusalem, Mary heard from Simeon, an old and holy man, that her heart would be pierced with a sword.

Mary, Joseph and the Christ-child lived together at Nazareth in peace and love. When Christ's public ministry began, when he was thirty years old, it would last just three years, and it would conclude with his death on the Cross at Calvary and the glory of his Resurrection.

Mary was with Jesus at his first miracle, at Cana in Galilee. It was a wedding. Mary saw that there was no more wine and spoke to Jesus. He gave her a puzzling reply, saying that "his time had not yet come". What did he mean? He was referring to his Passion and death. Mary pondered and trusted him. She told the servants at the wedding "Do whatever he tells you".

He told them to pour out the water from the great jugs that stood there—and as they did so they saw that it was wine.

Three years later, at the Last Supper, Christ used the word "do" again, the same word that Mary had used. He took bread and wine and he said "Do this is remembrance of me." He was establishing the Eucharist, and through this mystery he has remained with his Church through all time, never leaving us. The Wedding at Cana led directly to the Last Supper and to Calvary—and to our redemption when Christ died on the Cross.

We should follow Mary's advice and always "do whatever Christ tells us". She remained faithful right to the very end—standing at the foot of the Cross, a sword piercing her heart, close to Jesus and loving him just as she had done when he was a tiny baby or a small boy or a young man at Cana in Galilee at his first miracle.

After the great events of Christ's Resurrection and Ascension into Heaven, after Pentecost and the Apostles setting out to take the Gospel to the ends of the earth, Mary was taken up to Heaven by God. Faithful Christians will meet her there one day, and will understand fully the greatness of her role.

In Heaven we will all rejoice at the ultimate wedding feast. The wedding at Cana was a foretaste. In Heaven, all will be brought to fulfilment, and we will understand the full significance of the words of the bridegroom at Cana when he said that the best wine had been left until last.

Praying to Mary and invoking her aid and support is central to the life of every Catholic. One of the first prayers that we learn is the "Hail Mary", which opens with the words that the angel Gabriel spoke to Mary long long ago. The young Jewish maiden who said "yes" to God in response to those words of an angel made possible the redemption of the human race. The Church, like Mary, has to say "yes" to God, and brings God to everyone through the Scriptures and through the Sacraments.

In this book, we will explore the lives of some of the great women who have served Christ and the Church down the years. But the first and the greatest is Mary.

2

ST MARY MAGDALENE

ARY MAGDALENE IS one of the most popular and best-loved of all saints. She is mentioned in the New Testament as a great friend of Christ, and seems to have been the first person to see him after his Resurrection from the dead on Easter morning.

The name "Magdalene" may be because she came from the town of Magdala, but it may also be because it means "great" in Aramaic—it is essentially the same word as "magnificent".

Who was Mary Magdalene? In the Gospel of St Luke, chapter 8, verse 2, we read that "seven devils" were cast out of her. So she was some one who had been tormented by evil spirits, and who was released from these by Christ. Down the centuries, she has been portrayed as the most glorious example of a sinner who was cleansed and healed by Christ—a joyful and beautiful example for others to follow.

Was she also the Mary who is elsewhere referred to as a "sinful woman", perhaps a prostitute, who knelt before Christ in sorrow, pouring precious scented ointment over his feet? We do not know. She has often been linked to this woman, but there is no evidence, as the Gospels do not make it clear. Anointing Christ in this way was a prophetic act, because he would shortly die and women would come with herbs and spices to anoint his body.

She certainly became a devoted follower of Christ, and the most notable thing about her was that she remained with him right to the end, witnessing the Crucifixion, with Mary his mother and with St John. She is often depicted as kneeling at the foot of the Cross, weeping as Christ suffers.

On Easter morning she was one of the women who came to the tomb. And it was to Mary Magdalene that he appeared in the garden. "He appeared first to Mary Magdalene from whom he had cast out seven devils." (Mark 16:9).

In the Gospel of St John, there is an account of Mary Magdalene arriving at the tomb, finding it empty and running to tell the Apostles. She is distraught and bewildered: "They have taken away my Lord and we do not know where they have laid him". Peter and the Beloved Disciple run to the tomb, and Peter is the first to enter: "He saw and believed". Meanwhile Mary Magdalene was still weeping. Encountering some one in the garden, she assumed he was the gardener—but then he spoke to her. It was Christ, her beloved Lord. And he told her to go and tell the Apostles that he would one day ascend to his Father...

Surely there is a significance in this idea of Christ as the Gardener... there are echoes here of the original Garden of Eden : "And the Lord God planted a garden.." (Gen 2:8).

The account in St Mark's Gospel is a bit different: a group of women, Mary Magdalene among them, arrived at the tomb to find the stone rolled away, and a young man dressed in white who tells them to tell the disciples and Peter that the risen Lord will meet them in Galilee.

Tradition says that, after the great events of Pentecost, Mary Magdalene travelled with other members of the early Church and even reached France, where she helped to establish the Church: there has certainly been great devotion to her there down the centuries.

The name Magdalene in its various forms— Madeleine, Maddie, Maud—has been popular for Christian girls ever since the Gospels were first written. There are colleges at both Oxford and Cambridge named after St Mary Magdalene, and churches around the world. She has been depicted in paintings and in statues and in stained glass.

3

ST AGATHA

NE OF THE names of saints that you hear in the Canon of the Mass (Eucharistic Prayer 1) is that of St Agatha. Who was she?

Agatha was an early Christian martyr, who died in the days of the pagan Roman Empire. She was born in Sicily, and died as a martyr in about the year 251.

As a young woman, Agatha dedicated herself entirely to God, and vowed that she would not marry but would live entirely in God's service and in prayer. She was of noble birth, intelligent and gifted. The local Roman governor, Quintianus, who was from a poor family but had risen to high rank, wanted very badly to marry her. He was angered when she refused him, and was determined to humiliate her and force her to change her mind.

There are various stories and legends about what happened to St Agatha. At one stage, she was forced to live in a brothel, where the owner and her daughters were very cruel to her. Day after day she was subjected to threats and even tortures, and was urged to submit to Quintianus and to renounce her Christian beliefs and accept the Roman gods. Agatha refused. She could have saved herself by agreeing to Quintianus' demands, and could even have kept up her Christian beliefs in private if she had agreed to make some public gesture towards the pagan gods, but she refused to do this. She had pledged herself to Christ and she would not revoke this gift.

It is said that she was tortured by having her breasts cut off. One legend says that she was healed after a vision from St Peter.

Eventually, she was put to death by being burned on a bed of hot coals. Legend says that after her death an earthquake swallowed up Quintianus and his court, but we have no clear historical record of this.

St Agatha has long been honoured as a martyr, and although there have been legends about her, it is clear that she was a real person and that her martyrdom was well attested and publicly known. Her feast-day is on February 5th. She is the patron saint of women suffering from breast cancer, and also of breast-feeding mothers. Down the centuries there have been many paintings of her, including one showing her in prison with a vision of St Peter. Every year in Sicily there is a festival lasting several days around the time of her feast-day, and she is also honoured in the Basque country in Spain.

4

ST LUCY

THE NAME LUCY means "Light" (Latin: lux). She was one of the early Roman martyrs, dying for the Faith in the days when Christianity was illegal in the Roman Empire, and everyone had to worship the pagan gods. Lucy was born in about the year 283 and died in 304. She was a young woman of great beauty, and was a Christian, active in helping the poor and serving the Church.

A young pagan man wanted to marry her, but this would have meant publicly renouncing her faith so Lucy refused. It is not clear exactly what happened next. Some versions of the story say that he was so angry that he stabbed her in her eyes, making her blind and wrecking her beauty, and then turned her over to the public authorities and denounced her as a Christian so that she was executed. In some other versions, the guards in her prison put her eyes out. But none of these stories may be true—most of the legends seem to have developed later and the connection with St Lucy and eyes may simply be because her name means "light" and she has become associated with sight and being able to see clearly.

What is certainly clear is that Lucy was martyred for her faith, because she refused a pagan marriage and this was regarded as insulting and even idolatrous because it meant that she was putting her Christian beliefs before her duty as a Roman woman.

St Lucy's feast-day is on 13 December, at the darkest time of the year (and under an older calculation of the calendar, it marked the actual winter solstice, the shortest day of the year). She is honoured in Italy, and also particularly celebrated in Scandinavia (Denmark, Norway, and Sweden), where the winter days are particularly short and the nights long. As she is the patron saint of light, her feast is celebrated with candles in the early morning and in the afternoon of the previous day as dusk falls. Young girls dress up in long white robes and wear crowns of tinsel and evergreens and candles on their heads as "St Lucy angels". With the long white robe is a red sash, because St Lucy was a martyr.

It is traditional for a girl chosen to be a "St Lucy angel" to visit hospitals and residential homes for the elderly or for children with special needs, and to distribute small gifts and sweets. There are also candlelit processions honouring St Lucy, at which traditional Christmas carols and hymns are sung. The traditional food is "Lucy pastries", twists of puff-pastry with spices and dried fruit and melted sugar, enjoyed along with wheat germ and sugar in hot milk.

Because her feast-day is in December, St Lucy is very much linked with Christmas, and the coming of Christ's light into the world. The traditional white robe and tinsel crown of St Lucy is like the traditional robes worn by children dressing as Christmas angels in Nativity plays, or like the angel on a Christmas tree.

We hear St Lucy's name in the Canon of the Mass, where she is listed along with other early Roman martyrs. She is the patron saint of people who suffer from blindness or from eye diseases, and is also the special patron of young girls. There are churches named in her honour around the world.

5

St Clothilde, Queen of France

N THE STORY of France, the baptism of Clovis, king of the Franks, is central. It took place in the year 496, on Christmas Day. He was baptised by the Bishop of Reims, and afterwards he established a great abbey. Clovis' baptism gave France a place in the Church that has continued down the centuries: France is often called the "eldest daughter" of the Church.

Clovis' wife was Clothilde, and it was through her that Clovis came to know the Christian faith. Clothilde was the daughter of King Chilperic of Burgundy, and the marriage to Clovis was arranged to forge a strong new alliance, as he had just conquered the northern part of Gaul. They were happy together and had five children. But Clovis was uncertain of his faith: he accepted the beliefs of the Arians, who saw Jesus Christ as essentially simply a very good man but not as God.

Clothilde insisted that their first child was baptised, but sadly the child died not long afterwards. Clovis insisted that this was because of the baptism. The next child was also baptised, and when he too became ill Clovis was very angry. But the child survived and flourished, and the children that followed were also healthy.

Clovis faced various threats to his throne and in 496 there was a great battle against the Alamanii (from present-day Germany). Before the battle, Clovis made a solemn promise to God: if he was victorious, he would become a Christian. The battle did end in a victory and Clovis made good his promise and accepted baptism. His reign flourished, and he and Clothilde established themselves as a Christian royal family.

Clovis died in 511. Clothilde sought to establish the rights of her sons and grandsons to their family territory. She became embroiled in the battles and political campaigns that emerged. But eventually she retired to a convent. She established a number of churches and religious houses, including those at Laon, Andelys, and Rouen. When she died, she was buried alongside her husband in the great Abbey of St Genevieve, which he had founded after his baptism.

Today, as down all the centuries, there are French children named Clothilde in honour of this great saint and queen who helped to establish the Faith in their country.

In 1996 Pope—now Blessed—John Paul made a pilgrimage to France to mark the 1500th anniversary of Clovis' baptism. The following year he returned to address thousands of young people who flocked to Paris for World Youth Day. There had been much talk of the collapse of the Church in France, but the youth and vigour shown in 1997 gave a sense of new hope. Today, the Church in France faces problems, but there is still hope, as new movements emerge. The "eldest daughter" of the Church has a future as well as a past.

6

St Hildegard of Bingen—Wisdom, Music, and Cookery

CHOLAR, MYSTIC, COOK, VISIONARY, MUSICIAN — Hildegard was a remarkable woman whose influence is still felt today. She was born in 1098, into a noble family, and while still a young girl she was sent to live in a convent. She thrived there, and would spend her entire life as a nun, becoming an abbess.

As a child, she learned to play musical instruments, to study the Psalms and the liturgy of the Church, and to grow herbs and learn their uses. This last would prove to be a lifelong interest and would develop into a study of what today we would call biology and chemistry.

Hildegard was appointed as Prioress of a convent near the monastery of Disibodenburg. As Pope Benedict XVI noted in a discourse (General Audience, 2010) about her life:

> She fulfilled this office making the most of her gifts as a woman of culture and of lofty spirituality, capable of dealing competently with the organizational aspects of cloistered life. A few years later, partly because of the increasing number of young women who were knocking at the monastery door, Hildegard broke away

from the dominating male monastery of St
Disibodenburg with her community, taking it
to Bingen, calling it after St Rupert and here she
spent the rest of her days.

In due course Hildegard wrote a great deal of music
and poetry. In addition to her interest in the healing
properties of plants and minerals and herbs which she
studied in detail, she also herself seems to have had
healing powers, and once used water from the river
Rhine to heal a blind man. She wrote hymns, set
psalms to music, and even created a new alphabet
which she taught to the nuns in her convent.

At a time when public speaking and lecturing was
not something that women did, she became a noted
speaker, giving public addresses in churches and at
large convents and monasteries across her native
Germany. She corresponded with Popes and Bishops.
Her style was down-to-earth and she wrote with
fluency and confidence, and always with warmth and
charity. She challenged abuses in the Church, especially financial abuses, and was insistent on the call to
a simple and holy life in which members of a convent
or monastery lived in harmony.

Because of Hildeguard's wisdom, she was consulted
by rulers and politicians and she engaged in wide
correspondence with many of them. She was known
as one of the great intellectuals of her day.

Her ideas on the use of natural herbs for healing,
and the importance of wholesome food, has made her
popular among people today who are concerned about
overeating, obesity, and junk food. Because of her love
of learning she has been hailed as a role model for girls
at school and university. Confident and assertive
without being bossy, she saw men and women as

being partners and equals, both having a special and important role in God's plan for the human race.

In October 2012, Pope Benedict XVI named Hildegard a Doctor of the Church. She is one of just four women among the 35 Doctors of the Church. Pope Benedict described her as "an authentic teacher of theology and a profound scholar of natural science and music."

7

St Clare of Assisi

LARE—CHIARA IN ITALIAN—OFFREDUCCIO was born on 16 July 1194 to an aristocratic family. They were all devout Catholics, and her mother Ortolana had been on a number of pilgrimages including one to the Holy Land.

Chiara's parents wanted her to marry a suitable young man from a family they knew well. She asked to wait until she was eighteen, and they agreed to this. But when she turned eighteen, something dramatic happened: she heard the preaching of St Francis of Assisi, who had turned his back on the comfortable life of a merchant's son and had founded a community of friars living in radical poverty.

On Palm Sunday, all the local people, including Clare, went to collect palm branches for the big procession. She slipped away in the crowd and went to Francis, asking him to accept her vow of poverty as she wanted to live as he did. He cut her hair and gave her a simple black robe to wear, and she went to a convent of Benedictine nuns. Here, her father found her and begged her to return home to fulfil the plan for her marriage, but she told him she was committed: she wanted only Christ.

Later her sister Agnes joined her, and they established themselves in the church that Francis had built at San Damiano. This was the start of what was later to become a worldwide religious order, today known as the Poor Clares.

Radical poverty was at the core of Clare's understanding of the way they were to live. Owning nothing, and living in the simplest way possible, they went barefoot and spent long hours in prayer. Their life and its joyful commitment to Christ was to be an example to the world, offering a message of peace which could be shared by anyone and everyone who visited their convent. It was something radical in the church—and helped to give a renewal to the whole of Christianity.

Clare cared for St Francis in his last illness. She had always recognised his great spiritual gifts, and the message he had for the world. It is partly due to her writings that we know so much about the Franciscan way of life—its message of total, radical dedication to Christ.

Clare herself knew suffering because she was often ill, although she never complained and was always cheerful and a willing listener to the young women who joined the new Order. The advice she gave them is still followed today by the Poor Clares. She emphasised friendship, community, joy, kindness, and genuine poverty of spirit—with no pride or selfishness intervening to break the goodwill which should offer openness to all. Her letters give practical advice about how to live as a community, and lay great stress on the imitation of Christ.

On 11 August 1253 Clare died. She was canonised in 1255 and today there are communities all over the world who follow the Rule that she established, and are Poor Clares.

St Clare is the patron saint of television because, it is said, one day when she was too ill to attend Mass, she had a vision of the Mass on the wall of her room. It is perhaps suitable that an international Catholic television network, EWTN, was founded by a Poor Clare nun, Mother Angelica.

8

ST ELISABETH OF HUNGARY

ORN IN 1207, Elisabeth was the daughter of King Andrew of Hungary, and from the time she was a small girl, she knew that she would have great public duties to fulfil. Her parents planned that she would marry Ludwig, the ruler of Thuringia in the eastern part of Germany, because this would seal a strong alliance between the territories. When she was twelve, she was sent to live with Ludwig's family at the royal court of Thuringia, and when she was old enough, the marriage took place.

From the start, they wanted their marriage to be a truly Christian one. Although their wedding, as a Royal event, was marked with splendour, they deliberately did not have an elaborate wedding-banquet but instead arranged for the money to be spent on food for the poor.

The couple were very happy together: they knew one another well from childhood and as man and wife they loved each other. They had three children and all seemed set for a bright future.

Elisabeth was very devout: she learned about the teachings of St Francis of Assisi and his dedication to poverty, and she sought to live this way with great generosity and sincerity. She carried out many projects for the poor, and gave away large amounts to charity.

He husband warmly supported her and they worked together to foster goodwill and peace in the lands that he ruled.

Pope Benedict XVI, in a talk given about St Elisabeth (2010), relates a moving story:

> With her profound sensitivity, Elizabeth saw the contradictions between the faith professed and Christian practice. She could not bear compromise. Once, on entering a church on the Feast of the Assumption, she took off her crown, laid it before the Crucifix and, covering her face, lay prostrate on the ground. When her mother-in-law reprimanded her for this gesture, Elizabeth answered: 'How can I, a wretched creature, continue to wear a crown of earthly dignity, when I see my King Jesus Christ crowned with thorns?

Elisabeth is known as "Elisabeth of the roses" because of a miracle: one day when her husband was out hunting with a party of nobles from the castle, they came across Elisabeth who was on an errand of mercy to the poor. She was carrying some loaves of bread under her cloak, but some of the nobles thought she might be carrying away from the castle treasures to sell for the poor—something which would have made them very angry. Ludwig asked her to open up her cloak and she did so—revealing simply a great shower of roses.

When a plague broke out, Elisabeth established a hospital right by the castle, and worked there every day nursing the sick. She gave away everything she had to help the poor, selling ceremonial robes and jewels and keeping nothing of any value for herself at all. When her husband's duties took him away, she administered the lands they ruled and became popular as a just and fair administrator.

But in 1227 tragedy struck. Ludwig went away to join the Crusades as a soldier. In Italy be became ill and, without ever reaching the battlefields, he died. Elisabeth was broken-hearted when the news reached her: she is said to have gone out into the forests weeping and cried out "It is as if the whole world has died".

With her husband dead, Elisabeth's position changed. The throne went to a cousin who ruled because Elisabeth and Ludwig's son was still only a small boy. There were disputes and she had to leave the castle that had been her home. Her faith, always strong, now became central. She made a vow dedicating herself wholly to God. There was strong pressure on her to remarry, to forge a new alliance with some other royal family, but she refused to do this, and as a result she was bullied and treated very cruelly by her relations.

Elisabeth now suffered very severely. In addition, she had placed herself under the direction of a very strict priest, Konrad of Marburg, who imposed penances on her that were almost impossible to fulfil, concerning what she should and should not eat and other restrictions. But she continued her work for the poor and she also supervised the education of her children, and made sure that they would take up their duties and responsibilities in the world.

Living as a Franciscan, Elisabeth had no comforts of luxuries. At Marburg where she settled, she built another hospital for the poor and worked there daily to relieve their sufferings. People loved her, and flocked to be with her. She inspired others to live as she did, and to take up the message of St Francis.

Elisabeth died at the age of only 24. After her death miracles were reported after people prayed seeking her intercession. She was hailed as a saint. Her kindness and generosity, her renouncing of all worldly comforts and her devotion to the poor set an example which women across Europe admired and honoured. She was canonised as a saint by Pope Gregory IX.

9

St Birgitta of Sweden

YSTIC, VISIONARY, FOUNDER of the Brigettine order, and a central figure in Medieval Christianity and in the history of Sweden, St Birgitta—Bridget or Bridie in English—was born in the early 14th century into a noble family which owned much land in Sweden and was important at the Royal court. Through her mother she was related to the royal family.

Birgitta was fourteen years old when she was married, in 1316, to another nobleman, Ulf Godmarsson. They had a large family—eight children, and it was a happy home. The king was so impressed with the way that Birgitta was raising and educating her children that he wanted her to teach other women too. As Pope Benedict XVI would note, centuries later, in a lecture given about St Birgitta in 2010:

> King Magnus of Sweden so appreciated her wisdom that he summoned her to Court, so that she could introduce his young wife, Blanche of Namur, to Swedish culture. Birgitta, who was given spiritual guidance by a learned religious who initiated her into the study of the Scriptures, exercised a very positive influence on her family which, thanks to her presence, became a true "domestic church".

Birgitta and Ulf gave a strong witness to the joy and companionship of Christian marriage. As Pope Benedict noted:

> Together, Christian spouses can make a journey of holiness sustained by the grace of the sacrament of Marriage. It is often the woman, as happened in the life of St Birgitta and Ulf, who with her religious sensitivity, delicacy and gentleness succeeds in persuading her husband to follow a path of faith.

Birgitta had always been deeply religious, and after her husband's death she devoted her life entirely to Christ and the Church. She travelled to Assisi, to learn about St Francis and the Franciscan Order which he had founded, and then to Rome, to seek formal permission to establish a new religious order, the Order of the Most Holy Saviour, which still survives: its members are known as Brigettines.

This order would have both nuns and monks, who would live in separate houses in one large monastery, and come together to sing the Daily Office. Brigettine nuns of this Order wear a special form of headdress, in which white bands form a cross and red dots mark Christ's Five Wounds. There is today a thriving Brigettine convent in Rome, in the Piazza Farnese, and there are also Brigettine communities in many other places including Birmingham in England, and Holywell in Wales.

Birgitta devoted herself to the poor and sick, and she also spread devotion to Christ by recounting visions she had had of him. Her description of him as a tiny baby, glowing with light, with Mary kneeling alongside and angels gathered around and singing, has influenced the Christian view of the Nativity for centuries, and Christmas cards today still depict the scene more or less as Birgitta described it.

Birgitta's visions, and her encouragement of prayer, hugely influenced people across Europe and spread the idea of a united Christian civilisation.

Accompanied by her daughter Catherine, Birgitta lived in Rome for some years. She was much loved in the city because of her care for the poor and the sick. She wore the simple grey habit of the Brigettine Order and spent long hours in prayer. Although she had been born to great wealth, she never in her adult life enjoyed any luxuries and always lived very simply.

She went on pilgrimage to Jerusalem, and then returned to Rome where she died in 1373. Her body was brought back to Sweden and was buried at Vadstena, where a large Brigettine community was then established which flourished for many years. Birgitta was canonised in 1391. She is one of the patron saints of Europe. Her daughter Catherine is also honoured as a saint, and is known as Catherine of Vadstena.

10

ST JADWIGA OF POLAND

Y OUNG PRINCESS JADWIGA — HEDWIG in German — was the daughter of King Louis of Hungary and his wife Elisabeth of Bosnia. She was born in 1374. While she was still very young, after her father's death, she inherited the throne of Poland, after a complicated series of arrangements involving her father's wishes and plans and those of neighbouring ruling families.

There was no provision for a queen in Poland, or in Europe generally, at that time. Monarchs were mostly male. So Jadwiga was crowned as king rather than as queen.

In 1386 Jadwiga, still not yet in her teens, was married to Prince Władysław of Lithuania, in an arrangement through which Poland and Lithuania would be united, and the latter would adopt Christianity. It was very much a political alliance. Earlier, while still a very small child, Jadwiga had been promised to another Prince, William of Austria, and she had spent part of her childhood at the Royal court in the Austrian capital of Vienna. But politics intervened and in the end her destiny lay with the union of Poland and Lithuania — a union which was to have far-reaching consequences.

While the politicking went on, and her husband, who was some years older than her, was involving in power struggles and securing the structures of the new kingdom, Jadwiga devoted herself to charitable work, helping the poor and building up the Church. There are all sorts of legends about her, and especially how she had to carry out some of her charitable work secretly, because of the disapproval of her husband and the factions at court. One story is that she gave a jewel from her sandal to a poor man, a stonemason who was working on a building near the royal palace. After she left, he saw that the print of her bare foot remained in the plaster where he had been working: today people still visit the place and see the footprint.

Jadwiga often prayed before a large black crucifix in Wawel Cathedral in Krakow. Legend says that Christ himself spoke to her from this Cross, urging her in her work for her people. Today, people still go to pray in front of what is now known as "St Jadwiga's cross".

Jadwiga's marriage to Prince Władysław was crucial in bringing Christianity to Lithuania. Following his own baptism, he supported missionary efforts across Lithuania, and large numbers of people were baptised. Old pagan ways were abolished and Christian churches built, but the Church was not forced upon people by threats of violence or death. Jadwiga herself sent chalices and vestments to the new churches that were built in the Lithuanian capital of Vilnius.

Because Poland and Lithuania were now united as one kingdom, the whole territory was safe from the threat of being overtaken by either Austria or Russia. Polish-Lithuanian culture flourished. Down the centuries, Jadwiga's reign would be seen by Poles as representing their right to have their own language and customs.

Jadwiga was still only young when she died in childbirth in 1399. Her baby daughter died too. Her tomb in Wawel cathedral attracts large numbers of visitors every year.

There are many stories about St Jadwiga—some relate to the idea that her marriage was not an easy one, and that she had really wanted to be married to her childhood companion, William of Austria, but con-sented to the dynastic marriage for the good of her kingdom, and then concentrated on loving her husband and building up a strong bond. Certainly she worked hard to achieve unity between the Lithuanian and Polish people, honouring the Eastern rite liturgies although personally being brought up in the Western tradition, and working with her husband to build up schools and universities especially for the training of priests.

St Jadwiga was beatified by the Polish Pope, the great John Paul II, in 1986 and canonised in 1997. She is a patron saint of women who hold public office.

11

ST JOAN OF ARC— THE MAID OF FRANCE

OAN THE MAID "La Pucelle", Jeanne d'Arc is a legend and a national heroine in France. When she was born in 1412 the country had been at war with England for decades, and was in a state of confusion and poverty. Large stretches of countryside had been laid waste by English armies. The French lacked leadership and the English were reaping the benefits of a divided country racked by factions and reduced to helpless internal squabbles while its people suffered and starved.

The young Joan, born into a farming family in the east of France, was 16 when she approached the local garrison commander, Count Robert de Baudricourt, and asked to go to the royal court at Chinon because she had a message for the Dauphin, the heir to the French throne. She would later reveal that at the age of about 12 had seen a vision of Saints Michael and Catherine who had told her that she had a mission and must save France.

In an extraordinary series of events, the young Joan persuaded the military leaders to allow her to go with them to Chinon. They were impressed because she spoke authoritatively about the military and political situation with calm certainty, predicting—as came to pass—a military defeat near the city of Orleans.

At Chinon she met the Dauphin, Charles, despite a subterfuge in which he hid among his courtiers so that she would not be able to pick him out easily. Ignoring everyone else, she went straight to him and knelt before him. When they spoke together, he sensed that she carried an extraordinary authority and finally agreed to her request for a horse, armour and a banner—which she specified had to carry certain Christian images—so that she could lead a French army heading towards Orleans, which was under siege from the English.

While she was on the journey to Orleans, Charles arranged for enquiries to be made about her. Reports that were brought back emphasised her truthfulness, devotion, chastity and strong adherence to the moral teachings of the Church. Leading the army, Joan insisted on prayer, and complete abandonment of foul language or lewd behaviour of any kind.

At Orleans, despite being left out of all the Army councils and discussions of battle-plans, Joan effectively assumed leadership and the French routed the English and raised the siege of the city. The French Army entered the city in triumph. Further victories then followed, with Joan insistent that Charles must be crowned as king at Rheims. This was achieved and she was in the cathedral to witness the sacred ceremony.

After this, tragedy struck when, partly because they did not follow Joan's advice, the French military leaders allowed victory to slip through their hands, taking part in various skirmishes and arranging truces. She was eventually captured by the English, and after being imprisoned in various places and subjected to much cruelty and humiliation, she was tried as a witch. At one stage she was asked if she was in God's grace:

a trick question, because to answer "yes" would be to be accused of heresy (since none of us can be certain that we are sinless in God's eyes) and to answer "no" would be to admit her guilt. Her answer silenced everyone and has become famous "If I am not, may God put me there; and if I am, may God so keep me."

Joan's trial was essentially a political matter, and the outcome was unjust and cruel: she was declared to be a witch and was burned alive. As she was tied to the stake she begged for a crucifix to be held up so that she could gaze at it.

Joan's complete dependence on God, her candour and courage, marked her out so that everyone who met her was struck by her character. She defied convention by wearing men's clothing—necessary because she was in the battlefield and had to wear armour—and she continued to do so in prison partly as a defence against molestation by the prison guards and partly because she had no other clothes. Her sense of authority and qualities of leadership were astonishing in a teenage girl, and she also had a dignity that enabled her to speak with men of high position in such a way that they listened to her and even obeyed her.

St Joan's story has baffled theologians and historians. It took a long while for the Church to disentangle the legends about her from the truth, and her evident sanctity from the aura of national enthusiasm that surrounded her story as the centuries went by and generation after generation of French told and retold the events of her life. She was finally beatified in 1909 and canonised in 1920.

12

St Margaret Clitheroe—The Pearl of York

ORN IN 1555, Margaret Middleton was just 16 when she married when she married John Clitheroe, a local butcher. They set up home in the centre of York where he ran his shop, and they had three children. These were tumultuous years in the religious life of Britain. King Henry VIII had broken with the Catholic Church and announced himself head of the Church of England. John Clitheroe was among those who were brought up in this church, but one of his brothers became a Catholic priest and he was personally supportive of Catholics and sympathetic to them. In 1574 Margaret Clitheroe became a Catholic. She became very active in the local Catholic community. It was by this time illegal to be a Catholic priest, and they had to go into hiding and celebrate Mass secretly. The penal laws were savage and to be a priest was to risk death.

The Clitheroe family home in York, in a street known as The Shambles, became a Mass-centre, and Margaret regularly hid priests there. An entrance was cut from the attic of the house through to the one next door so that priests could escape when hunters came. Margaret also taught children the Catholic faith. Her son, Henry, would later go to Rheims and be ordained as a priest.

Margaret was known as a good neighbour and a woman of kindness and generosity. She was good-humoured and cheerful, and her home was a place of hospitality and welcome. The family was popular and respected.

In 1586 Margaret was arrested and charged with the crime of harbouring Catholic priests. Her husband was distraught, saying "Let them take all I have and spare her, for she is the best wife in all England, and the best Catholic." Margaret refused to plead either Guilty or Not Guilty before the court. She knew that if a trial went ahead, her children might be forced to give evidence. They would be faced with the choice of either lying or of giving information which would mean their mother would be executed. They might even be tortured into giving evidence.

A slim, slight woman, Margaret had great inner strength. In prison, she was cheerful among the other women prisoners and seemed unafraid to die. She joked and was amusing—but also spent long hours in prayer and it was clear that she had no intention of renouncing her faith or of co-operating in any way with the authorities.

Because of her refusal to plead, she was put to death in a particularly cruel way: a sharp stone was place on the ground and she was laid on it, and then a heavy door was placed upon her and weights were placed upon it so that she was slowly and painfully crushed to death.

When she was told that this vicious death awaited her, Margaret begged only that she not be stripped naked as was first threatened, but that she be allowed to be covered. This was allowed, and it is said that she sewed the robe herself the day before she was due to die. Her other clothes were taken from her, and she arranged that her stockings were sent secretly to her daughter Anne, a message that she must walk as her mother had done. On the morning of her death she appeared cheerful and unafraid. She had spent the previous night in prayer. A group of thugs had been hired to carry out the torture, earning money for doing so. It was Good Friday.

The Clitheroe family were well known in York, and Margaret's death, and the courage with which she met it, make a great impact. She became known as the "Pearl of York" (the name Margaret means "pearl"). The death by crushing was not in fact a standard punishment for refusing to plead and seems to have been a deliberate misrepresentation of the law. After the sentence had been carried out, the Queen, Elizabeth I, wrote to the people of York saying that it had been a miscarriage of justice and that, as a woman, Margaret should not have been subjected to this torture. The local feeling about Margaret Clitheroe was so strong and the indignation so great that civil unrest was feared and Elizabeth pretended to have a sense of solidarity with her as a woman, and to suggest that the death had all been due to a mistake.

Margaret Clitheroe was never forgotten in York down all the years that followed. In 1970, Pope Paul VI canonised her as one of the Forty Martyrs of England and Wales. Today, a plaque commemorates her on the city's bridge over the river Ouse. The house in The Shambles is a shrine, run by the Catholic Women's League, of which she is a patron. Books and plays have been written about Margaret Clitheroe and there are schools and churches named in her honour.

Anglicans and Catholics are friends and there is a new sense of understanding. Two Popes—Pope John Paul and Pope Benedict—have visited Britain. Christians all try to work together to bring Christ to people who do not know him.

13

St Kateri
Tekakwitha

HE Lily of the Mohawks is the beautiful title given to St Kateri Tekakwitha, who was canonised by Pope Benedict XVI in 2012.

The story begins in the year 1656, in territory in America which is now New York. Back then it was rural open land, the home of the Mohawk tribe of Indians. A baby girl was born to a Mohawk chief and his wife, Tagaskouita, who was a Catholic of the Algonquin tribe who had been baptised and educated by Jesuit missionaries. The baby girl thrived in her early years, but in 1661 a terrible epidemic of smallpox spread among the Mohawks—many died and the child, who was left with bad facial scars from the disease, was orphaned. Adopted by an uncle, she grew up in a rapidly changing world as the Mohawks moved about from place to place and also came into contact with the growing number of settlers from Europe who were already starting to transform the continent of North America.

At the age of eleven she met Jesuit missionaries, and at the age of eighteen she sought instruction in the Catholic Faith. She was baptised two years later when she was twenty. Now she had a new name—Kateri or Catherine.

Kateri was not just an enthusiastic convert—she
wanted to do penance so that others among the
Mohawks would be converted too. She joined a community of Mohawk Christian women. They practised
very severe penances, and Kateri slept with thorns on
her sleeping-mat, praying at night for the conversion
of her fellow-Indians.

The Jesuit missionaries continued to instruct the
Mohawk women. They had learned the local lan-
guages and understood and respected the culture,
seeing in it spiritual insights which could open the way
to Christian belief. Two of the missionary priests wrote
about Kateri, impressed by her dedication to prayer
and her simplicity of heart. She had suffered much as
a child because her face was badly scarred from the
smallpox epidemic, which had also affected her eye-
sight. Now she seemed to seek more and more penances, to live a life of complete mortification, because
she wanted to be close to God.

Kateri made a solemn vow consecrating herself to
Christ. At a time when many of the settlers assumed
that Indian women were immoral and promiscuous,
her life of prayer and mortification was an impressive
and solemn answer, and one that was a reproach to all
who looked down on Indians or regarded them as
inferior people.

We know much about Kateri's spiritual life, and the
penances she imposed upon herself, because the Jesuit
missionaries wrote so much about her, and were
touched and inspired by her devotion and by the
spiritual impact she made on the other women in the
small community where she lived. These Mohawk
Christian women were seeking to live like nuns,

although in a completely different habitat from the great convents and chapels of Europe.

Because of her poor health—made worse by her constant penances—at one stage her Jesuit confessor urged her to take a rest for a while by returning to her own village and staying there for a season. But she refused, saying that although the refreshment would be good for her body, it would not be good for her soul, which would hunger for God.

Kateri died at the age of only 24, worn out by her penances. She was much-loved, and greatly mourned. Hours after her death, her scarred face was seen to have changed—it was now radiantly beautiful. Over the days that followed, several people claimed to have had visions of her, shining with light and holding a bright cross, saying with joy that she was on her way to Heaven.

As Kateri's story became more and more widely known, devotion to her spread, and in the nineteenth and twentieth centuries Catholics across the USA and Canada came to regard her as a special patron in Heaven. Native American Indians, in particular, were devoted to her. Many prayed for her intercession, and information was gathered about miracles attributed to her.

Kateri was beatified in 1980 by Pope John Paul, and canonised by Pope Benedict XVI in 2012 At the canonisation ceremony in St Peter's in Rome, many attended in Native American Indian dress, and the celebrations included Mohawk and other American Indian traditions. The "Lily of the Mohawks" is a shining example of the way in which the Christian faith brings out the best and finest in all cultures, and ennobles and refines their traditions and heritage. Kateri was a woman of courage, faith, and resilience, loyal to her people and cherishing them. They are proud of her, and all American and Canadian Catholics share this pride.

14

ST ELIZABETH ANN SETON

HE BAYLEYS WERE a well-known family in New York. They had been among the earliest settlers. When a child was born to Richard and Catherine Bayley in 1774, her position in life seemed secure. But they could not have imagined what her life would be. She would go on to have many adventures, and to play a unique role in the history of America, becoming the first canonised saint born on the soil of the USA.

Elizabeth was still a small child—just three years old—when her mother Catherine died. Her father remarried, hoping to provide his children with a kind stepmother. Charlotte Amelia Barclay, a member of the Roosevelt family, proved to be a kindly and loving parent. She encouraged the young Elizabeth to join her in some of the many good works she carried out through the local Episcopalian church, distributing food and clothing to the local poor. Five children were also born to the family. But the happy times did not last. Grave differences between Richard and Charlotte eventually led to a separation. Richard went to Europe to pursue further studies for his medical career. Elizabeth and her sister went to live with an uncle.

But in due course she was to have a home of her own: at the age of nineteen she married William

Magree Seton, a New York businessman. It was a
notable wedding: the officiating clergyman was Rev
Samuel Provoost, the first Bishop of the Episcopal
Church of New York. Happy years followed. The
couple had five children. Elizabeth was kept busy—in
addition to her family life, she kept up her work for
the poor and needy, bringing together a group of
like-minded friends for this work.

In 1802 economic conditions and the loss of some
ships at sea brought about the bankruptcy of William
Seton's business. He was also unwell, and a doctor
recommended a trip to a warmer climate. They went
to Italy, but fell foul of quarantine regulations and had
to stay in a bleak and unsanitary place for some weeks.
Here William's illness worsened and he died. Elizabeth
was left alone in a strange country. Her late husband's
Italian business partners were kind to her, and in their
home she experienced real Christian charity. They
were Catholics and it was her first encounter with this
faith.

On returning home to the USA, Elizabeth became a
Catholic. Always devout, she now found a whole new
depth and meaning to her Christian faith. Needing to
support her young family, she opened a school, but it
did not flourish. There was still much prejudice against
Catholics and on discovering Mrs Seton's religion
several parents withdrew their daughters.

There were some difficult years. But Elizabeth had
energy and was also keen to help others in greater need
than herself. Encouraged by priests of the Sulpician
Order, she moved to Emmitsburg, Maryland. Here she
founded a school for poor children - the first free
Catholic school in the USA—and began what was
slowly formed into a religious community. People

began to call her "Mother Seton" and eventually this was formalised as she took religious vows.

The school flourished and set an example to be followed by many others. Mother Seton's energy and faith enabled many difficulties to be overcome. But she suffered: two of her daughters died while still young, there were tensions and misunderstandings in the community, and there were daily practical problems relating to the building up of the whole venture.

From these beginnings, however, much flowed. Today, a number of religious congregations across America can trace their origins back to Mother Seton's work, and she is recognised as the pioneer in the network of Catholic schools that now covers the country. She died at the age of 46, in 1821.

During her life, Mother Seton had a deep devotion to the Eucharist, and to the Scriptures. She understood the reality of suffering, widowhood, and loss. She endured prejudice and suffered disappointments and setbacks. In the years following her death she was hailed as a saint and she was beatified by Pope John XXIII in 1963 and canonised by Pope Paul VI in 1975. There are schools and chapels dedicated to her across America, and a statue in St Raymond's cemetery, New York, showing her in bonnet and long dress, holding a rosary.

15

BLESSED MARIE THERESE HAZE– FOUNDRESS OF SCHOOLS FOR GIRLS

F YOU GO to St Philomena's School, a large Catholic girls High School in the London suburb of Carshalton, you will find a life-sized statue of a nun standing with open arms alongside a modern theatre and meeting-hall used for big school events.

She is Sister Marie-Therese, born in the eighteenth century, and St Philomena's is just one of the many schools and other institutions which owe their origin to her.

Jeanne Haze was born in Liege, Belgium, in 1782. Her family suffered in the French revolution, having to flee to Germany and leave everything—their home, their possessions, all that had once made up their family life. While in exile, Jeanne's father died. Because of her experiences, the young Jeanne came to understand that material things were not what mattered: God, love, friendship, loyalty, and caring for one another were the really important things.

She was still only young when she felt a a strong call to dedicate herself to a life of service to the poor and those in trouble. Along with her sister Ferdinande, she started a little school for poor children in Liege. Other young women came to join them and finally they asked the local priest to help them form into a religious community.

The local priest was a Father Habets. He was very supportive of their work with poor children. A local house had been made available to the Church, and it had been arranged that Father Habets himself would have it as his home, because he was living in a dingy garret which was cold and inhospitable. But seeing the enthusiasm and dedication of young Jeanne and her colleagues, and the needs of the children, he offered them the house, cheerfully accepting to stay in his old rooms.

When the local Bishop came to visit, he was very impressed with what the young teachers were doing. Father Habets, although very supportive of their work, had not responded to their requests to talk about forming a religious community. Perhaps he thought that it was just a girlish idea and they were too young to make this sort of commitment. However, with the Bishop, he found himself discussing the plan and in due course agreed to Jeanne's request to have a detailed talk about it. Jeanne and her colleagues were clear about their wish. Their determination, and the support of Father Habets, meant that the project went forward and by 1833 they were formally established as the Daughters of the Cross. Father Habets would remain a lifelong friend and supporter of their work. Jean took the name Sister Marie Therese.

And it turned out to be a great work: establishing schools for girls, initially in mainland Europe and then later in England and in India, visiting prisoners, nursing the sick, running adult education classes. By the end of Marie Therese' life, there were some 900 Daughters of the Cross, and just over fifty convents in various parts of the world

The Daughters of the Cross today still honour the original ideals of their foundress. Their website notes: "The title that Blessed Marie Thérèse gave to her Congregation is significant. She had thought about it for a long time and from the contemplation of the passion and compassion of the Crucified Christ she learnt a tender, generous love which led her to follow Him to the end, faithful to the Holy Spirit and alert to His call. It summed up all she understood of the dual ideal of sacrifice and service which is at the very heart of Christianity. Our Lord also reminded her that there was another dimension to devotion to his Cross - it was a pledge of victory over death. By it Jesus had brought about our Redemption. Its meaning is more apparent in the French, "Filles de la Croix" for it means "servants" as well as "daughters". All the Sisters wear a cross surmounted by a white crown. The young Jeanne and a friend saw a vision of this in the sky over Liege on the day the first small community was established, and took it as a sign."

In Britain, the Daughters of the Cross established a residential school for children with special needs (St Elizabeth's, Hertfordshire), a hospice (St Raphael's), and a hospital (St Anthony's) among other projects. St Philomena's School was founded by the Daughters of the Cross and is now run by lay staff under the local diocese (Southwark).

Sister Marie Therese died in January 1876, the same year as Canon Habets, who had helped to get the Daughters of the Cross established. The work lives on.

And the author of this book about Saints and Heroines for girls is just one of thousands of women who have cause to be grateful to Sister Marie Therese: I was a pupil at St Philomena's. We had a portrait of her hanging in the hall where Morning Assembly was held every day, but I didn't know who she was. I am so glad to have learned her life-story.

16

St Mary McKillop— Heroine of the Australian Bush

ORN IN 1842 in Fitzroy in Victoria, Mary McKillop is the first native-born Australian saint. Her parents were impoverished Scots who had settled in Australia and who married in 1840 and had eight children of whom Mary was the oldest. By her own account, her home life was unsettled and unhappy—her father was affectionate and kind, but he seems to have found it impossible to find or retain a job, and at 14 Mary became the family breadwinner. She worked as a teacher, and then settled with an uncle and aunt as governess to their children on a farm in South Australia.

Always concerned to help others, Mary invited local children of poor settlers to join the lessons she was giving, and thus began a lifetime of service to education. In due course she moved back to Victoria and taught at a school in Portland, where she was also able to provide a home for her family. Father Woods, a South Australian priest who had been impressed with her work, arranged for her to return to help found a school. This she did, along with two of her sisters, using a stable which was adapted for the purpose by one of their brothers.

Mary's faith and sense of service was deepening all this time. There was a specific need to help the children of poor farmers in the bush country. With the encouragement and support of Father Woods, she made a vow of dedication to God, starting wearing a simple black gown, and in due course , at the age of just 25, made vows and became the founder of the Sisters of St Joseph, a new religious order. They settled at a convent in Adelaide. The purpose of the Sisters was the education of the children of the poor.

The Sisters—by 1867 they were ten in number— wore a brown habit and lived in poverty. They became known as the "Joeys" and became widely known and loved. They founded school after school out in the countryside, sharing the living conditions and hardships of the other settlers, in South Australia and Queensland. By 1871 the number of sisters had expanded to 130, and in addition to schools they ran homes for orphaned and abandoned children, a reform school, and a care home for the aged.

But this expansion brought tragedy in its wake—a series of complicated disputes brought a clash with the local Bishop who, acting on false information given by people who had started a campaign against her, excommunicated Mother McKillop, an action which resulted in the closure of most of her schools and the apparent destruction of all her work and plans. It also made her homeless as she could not longer claim her place in the convent—she was given hospitality and friendship by a Jewish family. She never spoke out against the Church or attempted to stir up public opposition to the Bishop.

Two years later, on his deathbed, the Bishop recognised that a grave error had been made and fully restored Mother McKillop in the Church. She went to Rome to regularise the position of the Order, and on her return was unanimously elected Superior General in 1875.

The Order's work expanded, and the Josephite schools flourished, but Mother McKillop's own sorrows were not over: there was a disagreement with Father Woods as he felt that the final version of the Order's Rule, approved by Pope Pius IX, was not faithful to the original form, and later there were problems with local bishops who disagreed with some of the educational policies of the sisters.

Mother McKillop suffered from poor health throughout her life, but continued with extensive travels to all the various projects run by her Order despite the hardships involved. This was pioneer Australia—rough tracks instead of roads, uncertain supplies of water in the heat, long distances to cover between settlements. In the days before telephones or internet, communication was slow, and handwritten letters were the chief method of sending news and instructions.

Opponents of Mother McKillop within the Church spread stories against her: that she drank, that she was disobedient to her Bishop, that she was obstinate and difficult with colleagues. In fact she was known to be a loyal and trustworthy woman, popular with her nuns and much-loved by school pupils and their parents. She always behaved correctly with her bishop and with all those in authority in the Church, while quietly insisting on her duties and obligations as the superior of a religious order with a clear rule and with work to do. Doctors had prescribed occasional glasses of wine to help relieve extreme pain cause by dysmenorrhea, an embarrassing and humiliating complaint which meant that she was sometimes bedridden. She continued working from her bed and also when travelling, and never allowed her illness to prevent her from tackling difficult issues or facing tough decisions.

Mary McKillop was known for her courage and her good humour. Often humiliated by senior clergy who were irritated by the fact that her Order was independent and not under their direct control, she continued her work with goodwill. By the 1890s there were Josephite schools across Queensland and South Australia and the Order expanded to New Zealand, where Mother McKillop spent a year working and travelling.

One of Mother McKillop's great supporters was Emmanuel Solomon, a former convict from London who became a successful businessman and Parliamentarian in South Australia. Thanks to his generosity and that of other non-Catholics, together with that of many people within the Church, Mother McKillop was able to keep expanding the range of her Order's work and the number of schools. She did not accept Government money for her schools, and was always anxious that they should serve the poorest children.

Mother McKillop died in 1909 and many regarded her as a saint. After the burial in a cemetery in Sydney, people frequently visited the grave and took away a small handful of earth as a relic. Eventually the body was exhumed and placed in a vault in a chapel in Sydney. The vault was a gift from a Presbyterian lady who was an admirer of Mother McKillop's life and work. Many people flocked to pray at the vault, and proceedings were begun to have Mary McKillop declared a saint. She was beautified by Pope John Paul in a massive outdoor ceremony on his visit to Australia in 1995, and canonised by Pope Benedict XVI in Rome in 2010, with some 8,000 Australians flying to Rome for the ceremony.

Mary McKillop has had a rose named in her honour, and a stamp created by Australia Post. An electoral district in South Australia bears her name, and there are several schools and colleges named after her. The "brown Joeys" have educated generations of Australians.

17

ST JOSEPHINE BAKHITA

I T WAS 1877. The little girl in the slave market in Sudan was so frightened and miserable that she did not even know her own name. Taken brutally from her home and family, and force-marched many miles to a strange place, sleepless, beaten, and terrified, she was in a state of shock.

And her life would get worse. Over the next years, she was sold and then re-sold, as if she was a horse or a donkey, to be used for work. She was flogged — and would bear the terrible scars for the rest of her life — and tortured by having cuts made to her skin and salt rubbed in to them, so that parts of her body were covered with elaborate patterns simply for the whim of her owners. She was starved and denied rest. When one set of owners had no further use for her, she was sold on. Faint memories of her mother and father, and of her long-ago life, receded further and further into the background. She would never be able to recall her original name. One group of owners called her "Bakhita", meaning "favoured one", so she stuck with that.

One day in Khartoum, the capital of Sudan, every-thing changed. Bakhita was bought by the Italian consul, Callisto Legnani. She was taken to the family home, where the Legnanis treated her not as a slave

but as a human being. They gave her care and affection, helped her to regain her health, and made it clear
that they would never allow her to be ill-treated again.
For the first time in years, she experienced gentleness
and friendship, and was able to talk a little about her
experiences and about her faint memories of childhood.

In 1884, the Legnanis had to leave Khartoum, and
return to Italy: they took Bakhita with them. They were
friends with another Italian family who had also been
in Khartoum, the Michielis, and in due course Bakhita
went to live with them, at the special request of Mrs
Michieli, who was expecting a child. Bakhita became
a much-loved nursemaid to the new baby, and a
valued member of the household.

When the Michieli family business meant that they
would once again have to leave Italy and live abroad,
they entrusted their child, Mimmina, and Bakhita, to
the local nuns. Here, Bakhita learned for the first time
about God. Hungry for more knowledge and information, she was fascinated by the Christian faith and
begged to be allowed to join a catechism class. She
loved it — and in due course received baptism. Years
later, she would kiss the font where she was baptised,
saying "Here I became a daughter of God." She took
a new name in baptism: Josephine.

When the Michielis returned to Italy they found that
Josephine Bakhita had matured. She was now a confident young woman. And she had just one great
longing — to remain in the convent and join the Sisters,
making her home there with them for life.

Josephine Bakhita was not a slave in Italy: as soon
as she had left Sudan and set foot on Italian soil, she
had become free, as Italy did not allow slavery. She
had lived with the Michielis willingly, and they had

given her affection and a sense of belonging. They were now rather hurt that she did not want to return to them. But she was quietly insistent: God was calling her and she wanted to spend the rest of her life with him as a Sister.

Taking religious vows in due course, Mother Josephine Bakhita lived quietly and happily at the convent of the Canossian Sisters. It was to be her home for nearly fifty years. The local people loved her. She sometimes spoke at church conferences and public events, explaining about her life as a slave and the joy and peace that she had found in Christ. Through her witness, more and more people came to know of the horror of slavery, and understood how cruel it was, and how necessary it was that it should be stamped out. But her message was one of peace and forgiveness. Once she was asked what she would do if she was ever faced with her captors: she said that she would kneel and kiss their hands in gratitude, because through them she had come to know and love Jesus Christ.

Mother Bakhita worked humbly and busily at the convent: she cooked and sewed and did housework, and she was particularly happy to be in charge of answering the door and welcoming people. The local children loved her: she would caress their faces and speak to them in her warm and comforting voice. People came to the convent to ask for practical help if they were poor or sick—but increasingly they came just to be greeted by her and to ask her advice about everyday family problems or have a word of cheer from her. She was always patient and kind, and always wanted to communicate the love of God, and the joy that she had found in learning about him.

In her last illness, Mother Bakhita suffered and her mind went back to her early terrible experiences of slavery. She begged the nurse "Please, please can you loosen these chains just a little? They are so heavy!" But at the end she was free from pain, and smiled radiantly as she repeated joyfully "Our Lady! Our Lady!" and even seemed to see her.

When she died in 1947, she was widely mourned. Everyone who knew her spoke of her as a saint. She was beatified in 1992 canonised by Pope John Paul II in 2000. Pope Benedict XVI related her life story in his encyclical *Spe Salvi*, as an example of Christian hope.

When Josephine Bakhita was first declared Blessed, the government of Sudan would not allow the news to be broadcast in that country. But Pope John Paul— defying advice which said that it was too dangerous— made a visit to Sudan. He was greeted with enthusiasm, and before a great crowd in the capital city he spoke about their saint: *"Rejoice, all of Africa!* Bakhita has come back to you. The daughter of Sudan sold into slavery as a living piece of merchandise and yet still free. Free with the freedom of the saints."

18

St Faustina Kowalska

ELENA KOWALSKA WOULD become famous and loved as Faustina, the name she took when she became a nun. Born in 1905 in the village of Glogowiec, then in the Russian Empire, she was one of ten children. Her parents were poor—her father was a carpenter—and the family lived very simply. They were devout Catholics, and from an early age Helena felt a calling to be a nun. But it was not possible—as a teenager she went out to work as a housekeeper in the nearby town of Łódź, sending her earnings back home where they were badly needed.

But when she was 19 she had a dramatic moment at a dance, with an overwhelming sense that Christ was calling her to be a Sister. Without telling her parents, she went to Warsaw by train the next day and made her way to a church. She had no contacts of any kind, but finally spoke to a priest who asked a local woman to give her a room while she sought out a convent.

After going to several convents, Helena found that it seemed unlikely that she would be welcomed anywhere: at that time, it was expected that a nun would have some education, and perhaps even bring a dowry with her. The only possibility was to work to save up a little money and then enter as a "lay sister", working at the cooking and cleaning. She was happy to do this, and was accepted by the Convent of Our Lady of Mercy. To earn the necessary money, she worked for a year as a housemaid, sending funds to the convent month by month. Finally, she was able to enter and take her vows, and her family attended the ceremony.

She worked cheerfully and willingly at the convent, but it was soon discovered that she was not well, with a persistent cough, and she was sent to another convent out in the countryside for fresh air and rest. When she seemed better, she returned to the convent at Plock, and it was there that, one night, she had a vision of Christ. Robed in white, he had rays of red and white light pouring from his heart. He told her: "Paint an image according to the pattern you see, with the signature: "Jesus, I trust in you." I desire that this image be venerated, first in your chapel, and then throughout the world. I promise that the soul that will venerate this image will not perish."

Over the next years, Christ would appear to Sister Faustina many times, and always his message was about his mercy—the great love and mercy that he had for the whole world. He asked that the first Sunday after Easter be established as Divine Mercy Sunday.

It was no easy thing for a girl from a peasant family, who had only with difficulty been accepted as a nun, and was in poor health, to tell her confessor that she had had visions of Christ and that he had given her a special mission of spreading the message of his Divine Mercy. Naturally, there was an assumption that she was unstable, or having hallucinations. Her confessor insisted that she be given a full psychiatric examination. The verdict was that she was absolutely normal and of sound mind.

Working in the bakery and in the garden, fulfilling all the duties allotted to her, Sister Faustina lived as an ordinary nun and never sought to draw attention to herself. The visions continued and, under obedience, she kept a diary of them. She noted carefully Christ's specific instructions, and also understood that this honouring of his Divine Mercy would not be something easy. At one stage she noted that there would be a time when the whole devotion was suppressed and that it would appear to be absolutely crushed, but then God would ensure that it was brought to fruition in a very special way, because it was something that had always been present in the Church but had been dormant.

In 1935 and 1936 the Devotion to the Divine Mercy finally became public, and over the next years it spread across Poland as various parishes took it up. There were booklets and pamphlets, and the picture that had been painted following Christ's request to Sister Faustina was reproduced widely.

In October 1938 Sister Faustina died. She had been a nun for just thirteen years, and had suffered illness for much of that time, eventually dying of tuberculosis. The sisters at the convent, just outside Krakow, kept the original picture in the convent chapel and encouraged people to pray there. By the start of World War II devotion to the Divine Mercy was popular in Poland, and during the war and in the years immediately afterwards, it spread rapidly, giving inspiration and hope to people suffering first under the Nazis and then under the new Communist regime. But in the 1950s it faced opposition in Rome: Sister Faustina's diary was placed on an Index of Forbidden Books and in 1959 devotion to the Divine Mercy was officially banned.

However, in the 1960s a new Archbishop of Krakow was appointed, Karol Wojtyła, and he was aware that the information given to Rome had been inaccurate and confused. The problem had been made worse because of the impossibility of proper communication between Rome and Poland during the Communist era. Eventually, in the 1970s, he succeeded in getting the ban lifted, and meanwhile Pope Paul VI had abolished the Index of Forbidden Books. A new chapter was opening. Sister Faustina's prediction was coming true: the Divine Mercy, always part of the Church, would now become honoured worldwide.

In 1978 Archbishop Wojtyła became Pope. One of his first encyclicals was on the Divine Mercy. In 1993 Sister Faustina was declared Blessed and in the year 2000 she was canonised—the first saint of the twenty-first century. Divine Mercy Sunday is now celebrated across the world on the first Sunday after Easter, and millions of people follow the Divine Mercy devotions. Pope John Paul called it "the appropriate and incisive answer that God wanted to offer to the questions and expectations of human beings in our time, marked by terrible tragedies". As Sister Faustina had predicted, the devotion had been crushed for a time but had then emerged more strongly than ever. She could never have imagined a Polish Pope, let alone one who made the huge impact that John Paul II—now himself Blessed John Paul II—made.

The Divine Mercy shrine on the outskirts of Krakow now attracts large numbers of pilgrims. A great modern church accommodates crowds for big occasions, and every day the modest chapel where Sister Faustina prayed is full for Mass and devotions. The message of Divine Mercy is a rich part of the life of the Church.

19

BLESSED NATALIA TUŁASIEWICZ

ATALIA TUŁASIEWICZ WAS a heroine of the Polish Resistance in World War II. Poland was invaded by Nazi Germany on 1 September 1939. On 3 September Britain declared war on Germany. But it was not possible to get any immediate help to the Poles. The Polish Army and Air Force were crushed by the Nazi war machine. The Nazis incorporated part of Poland into the Reich and the Polish people living in that territory were thrown out of their homes. The central part of Poland was termed the General Government area and was under Nazi occupation. And the east of the country had been invaded by the Soviet Union on 17 September, and people there faced the horror of Communist rule, with many people taken from their homes and sent under brutal conditions to the far north of the Soviet Union—many died on the way.

Natalia was born in Rzeszów on 9 April 1906. In 1921 the family moved to Poznań. She studied at Poznań University and after obtaining her degree she worked as a teacher. A devout and enthusiastic Catholic, she became active in a number of projects for local people run by church groups.

After the invasion in 1939, Natalia and her family were forced out of their home with just a few hours'

notice. The Germans closed all places of higher education and arrested professors and staff at Poland's
universities. Poles organised a complete "Underground State", with schools and even university
courses, and Natalia became involved in these. She
was also a leader in Catholic activity, teaching the
Faith, organising practical help for people in special
need, and encouraging people to pray together .

Over a million children were educated in Poland's
"underground schools" in defiance of the Nazis, and
some 10,000 people attended university courses. It was
too dangerous to award certificates, so instead stu-
dents who successfully passed exams were given
coded letters which, it was planned, could be
exchanged after the war for a valid diploma. Lessons
were given in private homes: everything had to be kept
secret and the teachers were usually just known by
code-names.

During these war years groups of Polish men and
women were regularly rounded up and sent to work
in Germany as forced labour. When a group of women
in Krakow, where she was then living and working,
were rounded up, Natalia volunteered to go with
them. As a teacher and as the leader of Catholic
activities, she felt that her place was with them . She
became an inspiration to the women, and when it was
discovered that she had volunteered to be with them
she was arrested, tortured, and condemned to death.
She was sent to the Ravensbruck concentration camp.
Her fellow-prisoners would afterwards remember her
climbing up on to a stool on Good Friday in 1945 and
speaking to them about the Passion and Resurrection
of Christ. Two days later she was taken to a gas
chamber and killed. It was Easter Sunday, 31 March

1945. The Allied armies were drawing near and reached Ravensbruck just 48 hours after her death.

In 1999 Pope John Paul II declared Natalia Blessed. She is one of 108 Polish Martyrs of World War II.

20

ST EDITH STEIN

N YOM KIPPUR, the solemn Jewish Day of Atonement, in the year 1891, a baby girl was born to a devout Jewish family in Breslau in Germany (now Wroclaw in Poland). It was a warm and loving family, and the child, Edith, was the youngest of a large number of children. When she was only seven her father died, and her mother had to manage the family business and raise the children alone. Edith was very close to her mother and admired her very much, seeing in her the "strong woman" who is praised in the Book of Proverbs.

During the First World War Edith became a nurse and worked with courage and dedication caring for the German soldiers. She was patriotic and keen to serve her country. A gifted and intelligent young woman, she achieved a doctorate at the University of Göttingen and began to be known as a brilliant philosopher. She worked in the academic staff of the University of Freiburg. At this stage, she had been an atheist for some years, although she loved and admired her mother's deep faith. In 1920 and 1921 she came into contact with the Christian faith, impressed by Christian friends. She read and studied it in great depth, and on 1 January 1922 she was baptised.

Edith went to work at a Catholic girls' school and was deeply interested in women's education: this was at a time when opportunities for women were opening

up, and for the first time they could study for full
degrees and obtain teaching posts as professors in
universities. She sought to discuss and explore how
women could use their gifts and skills best in the
service of humanity, not neglecting the essence of their
femininity. She emphasised that girls needed to be
educated in ways that would equip them to develop
morally and spiritually as women, so that the whole
of the human community would be enriched. The
object should not be "success in a career" but a life
lived fully—life in the home and in the family, in the
workplace, in academia, and in public service.

In addition to her work in school, Edith maintained
her contacts with the academic world at university
level. But the Nazis were gaining power in Germany
and she was forced to give up a series of lectures
because of anti-Jewish laws.

Edith's own spiritual journey was continuing, and
she felt a strong call to become a Carmelite sister, and
dedicate her whole life to God. She entered the Carmel
in Cologne in 1933. This was a life of prayer in a
structured community, observing vows of poverty,
chastity and obedience. Her superiors encouraged her
to continue with her academic work, and she produced
books and essays on philosophical subjects. As a
counter to the anti-Jewish tide that was rising in
Germany, her Mother Superior urged her to write
about her Jewish family and childhood, and the result
was a beautiful book describing the loving atmosphere
of a devout Jewish home and the values that sustained
it.

World War II began, and because Jews were now
being openly threatened in Germany, Edith—known
now by her religious name of Sister Teresa Benedicta

of the Cross—was moved with her sister Rosa, who had also become a nun, to a Carmel at Echt in The Netherlands.

In 1942 the Catholic Bishops of The Netherlands issued a pastoral letter denouncing the Nazis persecution of the Jews. It was read out in all the Catholic churches of Holland. Angered, the Nazi authorities began a fresh round-up of Jews, including those who had converted to Christianity and who had previously been left alone. Edith and her sister were taken from the convent and herded, along with large numbers of others, on a train to a transit camp.

Back in 1939, Edith had written out a testament of her beliefs which affirmed her faith and announced that she was willing to give her life for the salvation of Jewish people and of Germany, and for the peace of the world. As she and Rosa were being taken from the convent in Echt, she told her sister "Come, Rosa, we are going for our people." She understood that this could be the sacrifice that she had offered to God, and she faced it with courage.

As a prisoner, in the transit camp where Jewish families were taken, she sought to help the distraught young mothers who were trying to care for their children, and did all she could to alleviate the suffering that all were enduring. Some who later survived recalled the way in which she gave courage and inspiration to people around her.

The prisoners were herded in due course on to cattle-trucks which were set on the long grim railway journey to Auschwitz in Poland. Here, in August 1942, Edith Stein and her sister were put to death in the gas chambers. The exact date is not certain, but is thought to be 9 August. The prisoners' bodies were not buried but were burned and the ashes scattered, and no memorial was kept.

Edith Stein was beatified by Pope John Paul in 1987 as a martyr. Through her, we can understand the horror of the murder of six million Jews in the Holocaust, each one a member of a family with a life, and gifts, and talents, and hopes, and achievements, and an ability to love and be loved.

Edith Stein's work as a philosopher greatly influenced Pope John Paul, and her writings on women's education are of great importance in the twenty-first century as a new generation grapples with the issues of how to combine family life with the workplace and with service to the wider community. She is also a figure who helps us all to understand the importance of a special bond between Christians and Jews. Her love for God, her appreciation of her family heritage and its spiritual depth, her understanding of the beauty and strength of a mother's role, and her personal courage in the face of imprisonment and death, make her an important saint for modern women.

21

THE MARTYRS OF
RUSSIA

I N 1917, A Communist regime was installed in Russia and the country was renamed as the Union of Soviet Socialist Republics. The principal architect of the ideas and policies on which it was based over the next years was Vladimir Illyich Lenin , who took his principal ideas from Karl Marx. Marxism-Leninism was to cause famine, misery, injustice and death on a massive scale over the next decades. A very conservative estimate of the number of people who died as a direct result of the cruelty of Marxism-Leninism is 15 million: they died in concentration camps, in remote penal colonies where they were subjected to forced-labour, they died of hunger after all the farms were taken over by the government and no one was allowed to buy food. Lenin, and another tyrant, Stalin, dominated the Union of Soviet Socialist Republics for decades.

Essentially, Lenin saw control over every aspect of life as crucial to the success of his project. People's homes and farms were confiscated by the State, along with the crops they had raised. There was starvation on a gigantic scale, and millions died of hunger — people tried to eat the bark of trees, and the straw from the thatched roofs of their cottages, and there were even reports of cannibalism. Any opposition to the

Lenin regime was crushed, and people were arrested, wrenched from their homes, and sent to prison camps in the far north beyond the Arctic Circle—where they died from hunger and cold—for alleged "crimes" which had no basis whatever in law, such as being presumed to be a "saboteur" or a spy, or failing to seem enthusiastic about the government. Children were taught to spy on their parents, and neighbours to spy on one another. People were forced to work, unpaid, on projects in mines or factories or canals that were not properly designed or had no real point, and then punished on a savage scale when the projects failed.

Children were taught that Lenin and Stalin were heroes. When Lenin died, his body was preserved and placed in a special place in the centre of Moscow and people were made to line up to pay homage to it. Christianity was seen as being in opposition to this worship of the new ideology: churches were closed, priests sent to prison, religious books and icons were destroyed. Anyone who objected was likely to be sent to prison. Torture was used to force people to "confess" to crimes they had never committed.

The 1920s and 30s in Russia have been accurately described as the years of "the great terror". There are unknown numbers of Christian martyrs from those years. The martyrdom continued through the 1940s and 50s. When Stalin died, it was finally admitted that he had been responsible for the slaughter of millions of people. Later it was admitted that Lenin was responsible too. Even in the 1970s the full truth was not being told—even though by then everyone knew that Communism had been a terrible project from the very beginning.

Today in Russia the full truth about those terrible years is being told—but only slowly, because so many families perished and it is necessary to piece together the tragic events of each one, little by little. There were husbands suddenly arrested at work, whose wives were never able to discover why they never came home. There were orphaned children roaming the streets, their parents having been taken away to prison camps, leaving them hungry and alone. There were teachers denounced by their pupils, dying far away in a forced-labour camp without ever knowing the reason for their sudden arrest and without being able to contact their families.

Most of their stories are unknown, but we know about some the Catholic martyrs of those years.

Mother Catherine Abrikosova was the foundress of a Dominican Order of sisters. Her story begins happily. She was born Anna Ivanovna Abrikosov in Moscow in 1883. The family was wealthy: they owned the biggest firm manufacturing jams and preserves in Russia, with branches in many cities. Her parents died while Anna was young and she was brought up by an uncle and aunt. She studied in England at Girton College, Cambridge, and later travelled in Europe. In 1903, she married a cousin, Vladimir Abriksov. She had been brought up an Orthodox Christian, but in 1908, in Paris, she converted to Catholicism, of the Eastern (Byzantine) Rite. With her husband, she had an audience in 1913 with Pope Pius X and they spoke to him about their hopes for Russia. Perhaps they dreamed of working to improve Orthodox-Catholic relations, and to put an end to the Great Schism that had lasted for nearly a thousand years. But things worked out very differently.

In 1913, having returned to Russia, Anna became a Dominican tertiary. She took the name Catherine, and became the leader of a small Dominican community of women in Moscow. The following year the First World War broke out, and in 1917 the Bolsheviks took control of Russia, seizing their moment with the misery and discontent caused by the war and the political turmoil as the Tsar was toppled from his throne and various groups battled for power. Marxism/Leninism was now to be the only ideology permitted in Russia.

Life was grim for everyone, but there were special problems for Catholics because, belonging to a world-wide Church, they could be seen as spies for a foreign power. From 1917, Mother Catherine—Ekaterina in Russian—had been the chief spokesman for the Catholics of Moscow. In November 1923 she was arrested for "assisting the international bourgeoisie" and for spying. She was sent to Tobolsk prison. Some years later, ill with cancer, she was released, but banned from visiting the main cities of Russia. She visited Moscow to discover what had happened to the women for whom she had care, and was re-arrested. She died in prison in 1936.

Because of her links abroad, Mother Catherine could have left Russia and found safety, but she deliberately chose to stay, believing that she should give witness to her faith in her own country.

In the small community she founded, there were other martyrs. Galina Fadeevna Jentkievicz was born in Russia, of Polish origin. She joined the Dominican community under Mother Catherine, taking the name Sister Rosa of the Heart of Mary. Arrested in 1923, she was sentenced to five years in prison and then "internal exile", banned from major cities. In 1944 she died from an illness in Kazakstan—a remote place where people lived in grim penal colonies—where she had gone to care for a sick sister. Like Mother Catherine, she had contacts abroad, including family in Poland, but stayed in Russia to remain faithful to her vows as a Dominican sister in some of the most grim times in Russia's history. Camilla Nikolaevna Kruszelnicka was a student in Moscow who became friendly with the Dominican community. She was arrested in 1933 and sent to a labour camp, was moved to a strict-regime camp in 1937 and shot there.

Today, following the collapse of Communism in Russia in 1990, there is a religious revival in the country and the churches are full. There is also renewed ecumenical hope, as for the first time in a thousand years, an Orthodox Bishop attended the inauguration of a Pope, with the inauguration of Pope Francis in March 2013. We can hope—and pray—that the sacrifices of the martyrs of the twentieth century will bear fruit in a New Evangelisation in the twenty-first.

22

THE BLESSED MARTYRS
OF DRINA

HE CITY OF Sarajevo played a major and tragic role in the events of the twentieth century. As the century opened the city was part of the Austro-Hungarian empire. In the summer of 1914 the heir to the throne of that empire, Archduke Franz Ferdinand, was shot here with his wife, the first spark in the great conflagration of the First World War.

Later, in the Second World War, this area was a centre of violence. In the nearby small town of Pale, a group of sisters, who had been running schools and catechism classes for local children, became caught up in the fighting.

The sisters had been active in the area since before the First World War. They ran a convalescent home which had a chapel attached. Although historically there had been great tensions between Catholics and Orthodox in this region, the Sisters were known and respected by everyone. Some of them had worked in a school at Sarajevo, others taught in local Catholic parishes, and their convalescent home, dedicated to Our Lady, welcomed anyone who needed help, whether Catholic or Orthodox.

The morning of 11 December 1941 was one of deep snow and bitter cold. There were five sisters in the community at this time, and four of them, Sisters

Antonija, Berchmana, Bernadeta, and Krizina were in
the house. There was an atmosphere of fear and
apprehension as gunshots had been heard in the area.
Serbian militants were around and the Sisters were
vulnerable. As Catholic nuns, they would be deemed
to be anti-Serbian. The leader of their small community, Sister Julia, was out in the town buying food. As
she approached the convent with the goods she had
obtained, she saw that it was surrounded by Serbian
militants. Anxious about her sisters she hurried inside.
The convent's caretaker, Franjo Milišić, was with her
but, sensing danger, she sent him quickly away, saying
that her place was with her sisters but she did not want
to put anyone else at risk.

The Serbian militants shouted at the nuns, and
forced them outside into the snow. They refused to let
them take any outdoor clothing with them. They
marched them to a nearby house and then set the
convent alight. Inside the house the owners, an Orthodox couple, attempted to protect the nuns but to no
avail. Their captors forced them out into the snow
again and made them start walking.

For the next four days, the sisters, in the bitter cold,
were force-marched some forty miles. Sister Berchmana, who was elderly, collapsed and they left her by
the roadside saying she would be collected later. The
other sisters were forced on. They were marched at
gunpoint across the Romanija mountain to the outpost
of Goradze.

Here, pushed into a room on the second floor of a
barracks, they were told that if they were prepared to
give sexual favours to the men they would be released
and could work as nurses. The nuns refused. An
onlooker remembers one of them shouting "We prefer

death to what you want!" They insisted that they were prepared to nurse the wounded and sick but would never give the men what they wanted. As the men shouted and pushed them, they prayed aloud and, seeking to escape, clambered out of the window. Landing hurt and stumbling, they attempted to run but were caught and dragged to the nearby river Drina, where they were stabbed to death.

No one knew what had happened to the nuns and the people of Pale were anxious to find out their fate. In the spring, some others sisters from the Daughters of Divine Charity began a hunt for them. They learned that elderly Sister Berchmana who had been left by the roadside, had been collected by some of the Serbian militants who told her that they were taking her to join her sisters. But the militants in fact murdered her, and her body was never found. One of the young militants was later seen wearing her rosary round his neck.

The Sisters' popularity locally, and the service they had given to the poor and sick regardless of religious affiliation, brought a wave of devotion to them. Over the postwar years this grew steadily. They were regarded as martyrs and as the details of their deaths emerged, they were hailed as saints especially because of their refusal to abandon their vows of chastity.

In 2011 in a ceremony in Sarajevo, the Martyrs of Drina were formally beatified in a ceremony led by Cardinal Angelo Amato, Prefect of the Congregation of Saints.

23

ST GIANNA MOLLA—
DOCTOR AND
HEROINE

N 2004, FOR the first ever in the history of the Church, a husband witnessed the canonisation of his wife. Imagine what that must have been like: hearing the voice of the Pope solemnly announcing that your wife is a saint, to be honoured in the Church's calendar, invoked by people across the world in prayer.

Gianna Beretta was born in 1922 and grew up in Lombardy in a large Catholic family—she was the tenth of thirteen children. She studied medicine in Milan, and qualified as a doctor in 1949. She worked specifically in the health-care of mothers and small children. In 1954 she met Pietro Molla, and they were married the following year. He was an engineer. They settled into a happy married life and had three children, Pierluigi, Mariolina, and Laura. They were a busy and sports-loving family—Gianna enjoyed skiing and they went on mountain holiday trips.

In 1961 Gianna was glad to discover that she was expecting another child. She had suffered two miscarriages, and so the news that this baby seemed healthy and would survive was joyful. But tragically, complications set in. Suffering from severe pains she consulted a doctor, and x-rays revealed a growth, a fibroma, in her womb. One option was to remove her whole womb—which would also mean, of course, killing the baby that she was carrying. A much more risky option was to remove only the growth itself. This would save the baby, but carried dangers for GIanna. She insisted, however, that there could be no question of allowing the child to be killed. She had the operation and continued with the pregnancy.

She continued to be unwell and to suffer pain. She knew that things were not going well, and she was realistic about what might happen. She told her husband "This time it will be a difficult delivery, and they may have to save one or the other—I want them to save my baby."

It was Good Friday—21 April 1962—when Gianna went into hospital to have the baby. A Caesarian operation was performed and the child was healthy and was safely delivered. But Gianna's condition worsened. She survived the operation but an infection set in and a week later she died.

Gianna's courage and faithfulness in insisting that her child be given the chance to live became widely known. She had been a popular doctor and was admired for the way in which she combined her medical work with care for her family, and for her strong and generous faith. Many families had cause to be grateful to her for the excellent medical care she had given to their children. And many women owed her thanks for the care and advice she had given them in their pregnancies.

Her deep and sincere faith was also well known: she had a strong prayer-life, and had a special and active concern for the poor and the marginalised. As she was dying, she was heard saying over and over again "Jesus, I love you".

As the years went by following her death, many people, especially women with problem pregnancies, asked her intercession as a saint. In April 1994 she was formally declared Blessed by Pope John Paul II, and in 2004 she was canonised: she is now Saint Gianna Molla. So far as is known, she is the first saint to have been photographed in slacks and skiing-clothes. Gianna Molla was in every way a modern wife and mother who enjoyed the good things that the twentieth century offered, including the opportunity for a woman to gain good educational qualifications and to train for a career. She exemplified the courage and strong-minded sense of fair play and justice that a believing Christian can show even in the face of suffering. She had no desire to die, and every reason to live—with a young family and a loving husband, a good career and useful skills that were needed by the wider community. But she would not deny her child's right to life, and she was prepared to take a risk in order to ensure that the child survived.

The Church did not force Gianna to carry the child to term. Because of the risk to her own life, Gianna could morally have had the operation for hysterectomy, but she deliberately asked for the alternative of merely seeking the removal of the fibroma, because she wanted to save the child she was carrying.

Today, St Gianna Molla is the patron saint of pregnant women and of young mothers. Her husband Pietro died in 2010 at the age of 97.

In his homily at her canonisation, Pope John Paul quoted a letter that Gianna wrote to her future husband when they were engaged: *"Love is the most beautiful sentiment the Lord has put into the soul of men and women"*.

24

BLESSED JACINTA MARTO—WITNESS TO A VISION

A LITTLE UNEDUCATED GIRL from an unimportant village in Portugal, who could not read or write, and had never been to school, whose life ended before she reached her eleventh birthday... how could she be involved in events connected with the great drama of the twentieth century?

Jacinta Marto was born in March 1910. She and her brother Francisco, together with their cousin Lucia, worked with their families who were farmers near the village of Fatima. All were Catholics and the children were well-formed in the faith. Jacinta was a bright child, who enjoyed singing and dancing. Lucia was older than her two cousins, an intelligent girl with an exceptionally good memory.

The lives of all three children changed utterly one day in 1917. They were looking after the family sheep, and were stunned by a sudden bright vision. Lucia would later describe it as a woman "brighter than the sun, shedding rays of light clearer and stronger than a crystal ball filled with the most sparkling water..."

It was 13 May 1917. The children had no knowledge of world events—in their corner of rural Portugal the drama of the great war raging elsewhere in Europe had passed them by. The lady in the vision spoke to them. She asked them to do penance for sinners. They understood her to be the Virgin Mary, and to be bringing them an urgent message from God. From that day on, they began to pray very seriously and to undertake penances. There were further visions, and when the children reported these, there was huge public interest. The children were taken by the police and repeatedly interrogated but insisted on the simple truth of what they had seen.

Our Lady told the children to come to the Cova da Iria—where the visions had been taking place—on 13 October where she would give them a special sign. Word spread, and on the appointed day, some 10,000 people crowded into the fields nearby. It was a day of pouring rain and people were sheltering beneath umbrellas. As the children knelt in prayer, extraordinary things began to happen, the sun appearing to spin in the sky and to send out brilliant rays. The rain completely disappeared. The spinning sun was also seen by people some miles away and was reported in the newspapers. The local authorities, which were very much opposed to the Church and to any religious activity, were stunned.

Lucia later recorded that the lady had spoken with some very specific instructions: there must be much prayer and penance, and people should receive Communion on the first Saturday of each month in reparation for sin. She said that unless people repented, another war would break out: "When you see a night illuminated by an unknown light, know that this is the great sign given you by God that he is about to punish the world for its crimes, by means of war, famine, and persecutions of the Church and of the Holy Father. To prevent this, I shall come to ask for the consecration of Russia to my Immaculate Heart, and the Communion of reparation on the First Saturdays. If my requests are heeded, Russia will be converted, and there will be peace; if not, she will spread her errors throughout the world, causing wars and persecutions of the Church. The good will be martyred; the Holy Father will have much to suffer; various nations will be annihilated. In the end, my Immaculate Heart will triumph. The Holy Father will consecrate Russia to me, and she shall be converted, and a period of peace will be granted to the world."

It seems that the children did not really understand all of this. They did not know that at that very time in Russia, an atheistic Communist regime was taking power that would bring savage persecution and misery to millions. Lucia simply faithfully committed to memory all that Mary said in the vision. But the children understood that it was to be kept secret and what was emphasised at the time was simply a call to prayer and penance. The Church, after repeatedly questioning the children, began to take this seriously. Pilgrimages began to the Cova, the Rosary was said, and a great devotion to "Our Lady of Fatima" began.

In the months that followed, the children lived an extremely rigorous regime of prayer. In addition to the message about Russia, they had been given a terrible vision of Hell, and also a very specific vision of a Pope being shot: these were all to remain secret until Lucia was given an indication that they should be revealed.

Both Francisco and Jacinta became gravely ill during the worldwide influenza epidemic that followed the First World War. Francisco died in 1919. Jacinta's sufferings were increased because she was moved from hospital to hospital and given a number of extremely painful treatments in an effort to save her life. She never complained and was heard repeatedly "offering up" her sufferings for the conversion of sinners. The child who had always been merry and light-hearted was now solemn, but never showed any signs of self-pity. Her loneliness in hospital was acute as she had never been away from her family before. She finally died on 20 February 1920.

Lucia, meanwhile, had gone into a convent. Taught to read and write, she set down a careful and detailed account of the Fatima visions. The first two parts of the secret—the vision of Hell and the prophecies about Russia—were published in due course. In the Second World War it all fitted together—the "night illuminated by an unknown light" seemed to refer to the extraordinary *aurora borealis* that was seen across Europe in 1938 shortly before the annexation of Austria by Germany that began the events leading up to the outbreak of war in 1939. The message about Russia seemed of huge importance as Communist rule there brought massive suffering: a vast cruel network of concentration camps established in the Arctic circle where millions died in horrific conditions of starvation and brutality. After 1945 formerly independent nations in Eastern Europe, including Poland and Czechoslovakia also came under Russian domination and lost their freedom. In the 1950s prayers for Russia and devotion to Our Lady of Fatima became a major part of Catholic life across the world.

In 1978, with Russia and Eastern Europe still in the grip of Communism, the Church elected a Polish Pope, John Paul II. On 13 May 1981 he was shot in St Peter's Square, and narrowly escaped death. He had dedicated his life to Mary, and prayed to her as he was rushed to hospital. As he lay recovering, he was struck by the fact that the assassination attempt had been on the anniversary of the Fatima apparitions, and sent for the sealed envelope which contained the last of the three secrets. In it, he read Lucia's description of a pope being shot, and recognised himself.

In 1984 he fulfilled Our Lady's request and consecrated the world to her Immaculate Heart, having asked all the bishops of the world to unite themselves with him in this. The consecration was also carried out in Russia itself, by a Ukrainian archbishop secretly in a cathedral open to tourists, using a newspaper spread open as a shield.

In his prayer in Rome, Pope John Paul specifically mentioned "those individuals and nations that particularly need to be thus entrusted and consecrated". This marked a turning-point. Communism crumbled and by 1990 it was over. The conversion of Russia began and continues: today the churches are full, new ones are being built, those that had been turned into "museums of atheism" in the Communist era are back in use, and a great Catholic shrine to Our Lady of Fatima has been built in Kazakhstan, the territory where some of the most terrible concentration camps existed. The country is still an unhappy place, with much hardship, but has begun an extraordinary spiritual journey.

In the year 2000 Jacinta and Francisco were beatified by Pope John Paul: at the ceremony the final secret was also revealed with its vision of the Pope being shot, a Pope who struggled over a ruined city with heaps of corpses. It was an all-too-accurate description of the horrors of the twentieth century and the suffering caused by atheism.

Both Pope John Paul and Pope Benedict have emphasised the continuing importance of Fatima — the essential message is about prayer and penance. Blessed Jacinta Marto, by humbly and faithfully doing what Mary asked, lived the message of Fatima to the full.

25

BLESSED TERESA OF CALCUTTA

GNES GONXHA BOJAXHIU—HER middle name means "rosebud" in Albanian—was born in what is today Macedonia, in 1910. Her father was active in Albanian politics. She was brought up in a happy Catholic family, in a home where there was affection and strong faith. Her father died when she was young and her mother opened a small clothing and embroidery business. The family was active in the local Catholic parish.

Agnes felt a strong call to religious life and to missionary work and at the age of 18 she left home to join a missionary order of nuns. She knew that this might mean she would never see her family again, but she could not have known that the Second World War and the imposition of a Communist regime in Albania would mean that all communication would be impossible for many years.

Joining the Loreto sisters, she was sent first to a convent in Ireland where she learned English, and then to India where she joined the teaching staff at one of the order's popular and successful schools. She had taken the name Teresa on her final profession as a nun. She taught in Calcutta throughout the late 1930s and early 1940s. In 1946, during a time of great unrest and suffering in India, she felt a "call within a call" to serve the poorest of the poor. She obtained permission to leave the convent and start work among the beggars and the destitute in Calcutta's slums. Gradually young women joined her, and eventually her new religious order, the Missionaries of Charity, was formally established.

Its work expanded steadily—first across India and then to other continents, opening homes for the destitute and dying, for orphans, for the frail and sick, and for the abandoned elderly. The sisters wear an Indian sari-style habit of white with a distinctive blue border. They take a special vow of poverty. Their chapels always feature a large crucifix beneath which is displayed Christ's words on the Cross: "I thirst".

Following a television programme in 1969 made by the British broadcaster Malcolm Muggeridge, Mother Teresa became a world-famous figure. Muggeridge—who subsequently became a Catholic—always spoke of her as a saint. Although much photographed and invited to take part in major international events and conferences, Mother Teresa retained her simple lifestyle, never omitting anything from her routine of prayer, maintaining her regime of fasting and hard work. She spoke out vigorously in defence of the poor and defenceless, and passionately opposed the killing of unborn babies through abortion, speaking of abortion as "the greatest destroyer of peace in the world." When asked about poverty, she would often refer to the spiritual poverty of the rich Western nations, with families split by divorce, lonely people left unvisited, and widespread abortion and contraception. In all her convents, she and her sisters lived in complete simplicity, without carpets, electrical gadgets, or any form of luxury.

Mother Teresa was awarded the Nobel Prize for Peace and in her lecture receiving the award she noted:

> Around the world, not only in the poor countries, but I found the poverty of the West so much more difficult to remove. When I pick up a person from the street, hungry, I give him a plate of rice, a piece of bread, I have satisfied. I have removed that hunger. But a person that is shut out, that feels unwanted, unloved, terrified, the person that has been thrown out from society—that poverty is so hurting and so much, and I find that very difficult.

Suffering from poor health throughout the 1980s and 90s, Mother Teresa nevertheless succeeded in opening homes across the world—including in countries with anti-Catholic regimes. She was finally able to open one in her native Albania once it was freed from Communist rule. Always responding to new calls and new demands, she opened homes for AIDS victims, and for the care of children orphaned through AIDS.

In 1994 Mother Teresa's native Albania awarded her the Golden Honour of the Nation. The country's international airport at Tirana is named after her, and her birthday, 18 October, is a national holiday. Over the years she was also honoured by many other countries: President Ronald Reagan of the USA presented her with the Congressional Medal of Freedom in 1985. India's fastest train is named the "Mother Express" to commemorate her.

By the time of Mother Teresa's death in 1997, there were some 4,000 members of her religious order across the world. The homes and orphanages run by the Missionaries of Charity are funded by donations from supporters, and gifts of money and clothing and food enable them to flourish. In addition to the homes and orphanages, they run schools for the poorest children, adoption schemes for orphans, soup kitchens and day centres.

Mother Teresa was given a State funeral in India, where she is regarded as a national heroine and where her grave attracts many visitors. She was beatified by Pope John Paul in 2003.

After her death, Mother Teresa's letters to her spiritual director and to other priests and friends were published and reveal that she experienced great spiritual loneliness, a sense of Christ being distant or simply not present at all. Her perseverance in prayer in this apparently empty spiritual desert is all the more remarkable.